Manuel Kröger

The Problem of Individuation in the Middle Ages

GRIN Verlag

Bibliografische Information der Deutschen Nationalbibliothek:

Die Deutsche Bibliothek verzeichnet diese Publikation in der Deutschen National-
bibliografie; detaillierte bibliografische Daten sind im Internet über http://dnb.d-
nb.de/ abrufbar.

Imprint:

Copyright © 2013 GRIN Verlag GmbH
Druck und Bindung: Books on Demand GmbH, Norderstedt Germany
ISBN: 978-3-656-52921-7

This book at GRIN:

http://www.grin.com/en/e-book/263751/the-problem-of-individuation-in-the-
middle-ages

GRIN - Your knowledge has value

Der GRIN Verlag publiziert seit 1998 wissenschaftliche Arbeiten von Studenten, Hochschullehrern und anderen Akademikern als eBook und gedrucktes Buch. Die Verlagswebsite www.grin.com ist die ideale Plattform zur Veröffentlichung von Hausarbeiten, Abschlussarbeiten, wissenschaftlichen Aufsätzen, Dissertationen und Fachbüchern.

Visit us on the internet:

http://www.grin.com/

http://www.facebook.com/grincom

http://www.twitter.com/grin_com

Ludwig-Maximilians-Universität München

The Problem of Individuation in the Middle Ages

Introduction to Medieval Philosophy

Philosophical Faculty
SoSe 2013
Author: Manuel Kröger
27.09.2013

Table of Contents

The Problem of Individuation in the Middle Ages

1. Introduction

This work is about how the problems of individuation and how it is discussed in the Middle Ages.

First I will give an overview about the core area of this philosophy and the problems of individuation generally: what does the term "individuation" mean and why does it lead to problems? What are the problems of individuation and how different philosophers tried to solve them?

Then I want especially show, what Aquinas is thinking about it.

Another point of interest will be where this question has its philosophical beginning.

I wondered first, as I picked up my theme for this work: how could there be a problem with individuation? For me, it seemed to be so clear what an individual is, how to distinguish several individuals. But then I realized: if you have to explain what it is that makes an individual an individual, the clarity becomes a complex web of ambiguities where more and more questions will appear, by proceeding to the answers of this philosophy. Many questions were asked and many attempts of solutions were proposed but every proposal is little satisfying.

We have to ask ourselves: What does it mean to be an individual? What makes me an individual? What makes the chair I sit on an individual? What makes me different from my neighbour? What, if there exists a second person in an parallel universe who is exactly like me: with the same appearance, the same abilities, the same name, the same behaviour, the same life story: a second me? Are we both individuals or are we the same person, because we are exactly identical? The answer is intuitively "no", but why we are not the same person? Is it because of the spatio-temporal individuation view?

Gracia denies this view:

The most commonly accepted view of accidental individuation is the one that holds it to be a result of spatial-and/or temporal location. The strongest version of this view is the one that (1) combines space and time into a single principle of individuation and (2) does not identify spatio-temporal location with external relation. The version of the view that does not combine space and time together is weak, for one could always object to it that distinct individuals can occupy the same space at different times or, alternatively, exist at the same time in different places. Similarly, the view that makes space and/or time an external relation is also weak, for then the individual's individuality would be a result of an external relation which would change no doubt with changing circumstances outside of it. Indeed, every time something moved in the universe, spatio-temporal location of everything else would be changed and presumably its individuality. The strongest view, consequently, rejects both of these approaches. It is spatial and temporal location, considered together and as non-relational and intrinsic, that must be used. [...] This view, however, has several problems. The first and foremost is that it attempts to explain what is a substantial feature of things (individuality) by reference to an accident or accidents (time and space).[1]

Here we have our first factor with is rejected by declaring an individual as individual: this cannot be made by presenting accidents. Accidents are nothing essential, though we often think of being individual by doing or wearing things which distinguish us from other people.

By researching the origin of the german word "Individuum" I found an interesting explanation:

Individuum s „der Mensch als Einzelwesen, die einzelne Person": Das Wort ist identisch mit *lat*. Indīviduum „das Unteilbare", das als LÜ von *gr*. átomos [...] mit verneinendem [...] *in...* zu *lat*. dīvidere „trennen, zerteilen" gebildet ist; vgl. *dividieren*. – Der in dem Wort zum Ausdruck kommende Wertbegriff, der den Menschen als einzelnen mit allen seinen Wesensgestimmtheiten einer Gemeinschaft bzw. der Masse gegenüberstellt, findet sich noch stärker in den verschiedenen Abl. neuerer Zeit ausgeprägt, so in: individuell „dem Individuum eigentümlich; von betonter Eigenart" (18. Jh.; aus *frz*. Individuel < *mlat*. Indīviduālis) [...].[2]

---

[1] Gracia, Jorge J. E. (1998): *Introduction to the problem of individuation in the early Middle Ages*. 2. Aufl. München [u.a.]: Philosophia-Verlag (Analytica), pp. 40-41.
[2] Drosdowski, Günther (Hg.) (1963): *Duden "Etymologie". Herkunftswörterbuch der deutschen Sprache*. Mannheim [u.a.]: Bibliogr. Inst (Der Duden in 10 Bänden, 7), p. 285.

Interesting is first of all that the german word "Individuum" – in English "individual" – just means a human person. This definition in this dictionary works especially for humans, not for other things. I think, this reflects the generally understanding of "individual". As opposed to this, the philosophers mean that every object, human or not, is an individual. They possess another understanding of this. But the definition of "Individuum" contains another, more important fact. It means "the indivisible". Indivisibility is a feature considered by many philosophers as important for an individual. I will approach this later.

But what are the notions of the philosophers in the Middle Ages? What can we learn from their investigations, questions, proposals and solution approaches? They had many of those but no approach seems to be sufficient.

2. The Problems of Individuation – Intension of Individuality

What are exactly the problems of individuation? Which questions we have to ask here?

There are an amount of problems and questions but I will just give an overview about one realm of this widespread field: the intension of individuality, based on the *Introduction to the Problem of Individuation in the Early Middle Ages* by Jorge J. E. Gracia, which is a very good piece of work about this theme. The intension of individuality contains, in my opinion, the most important questions and terms about the problem of individuation.

One of the biggest problems for the Medieval Authors, Gracia states, is to find the appropriate terms. No term seems to describe exactly the features of individuality without leading to misinterpretations. They all have "undesirable connotation[s]".[3]

In the philosophy of individuation are a big amount of different views from the different philosophers and thus it is difficult, to give a brief overview. But I try to manage this by listing not all different points of view but the principal ones.

---

[3] Gracia, p. 28.

One of the basic problems is to find a theory of individuation that holds for physics, meta-physics and non-substantial entities and for entities of the whole cosmos, disregarding the circumstances they exist in. So it has to apply for existing and non-existing entities. The individuation must inhere in the individual, not be an external but an intrinsic factor. So the properties of the individual make it individual not its accidents.

Gracia presents common intuitions we have about individuals:

> [They] (a) lose their fundamental character if they are divided into parts, (b) are distinct from all other entities, even from those that are of their same specific kind, (c) are one of a group type or class which has or can have several members, (d) remain the same through time and various changes, and (e) are not predicated of other things.[4]

Of course we aren't aware of this in this differentiated manner, but subconsciously we recognize these features as making the entities individual. But it is much more complicated than this, when we want to explain why exactly one entity is individual. What are the features of individuality?

In our world, in our reality, we can deal with the individuality. We mostly have no big problems to distinguish entities from each other. So, "what makes these intuitions the subject of philosophical reflection and interest is not just their immediacy, but their possible conflicts."[5]

First, we have to differentiate between individual entities, accidents, groups, species and genus.

> The specific nature consists of the common features which are part of what distinguishes the thing from a larger group or a kind of things and at the same time makes it part of a smaller group of things, the members of which can be distinguished only in terms of individual features. [...] The features that all members of several species have in common and which make them belong to a larger group which is in turn distinct from other larger groups, constitute the genus or generic nature. Both generic and specific features are essential to the thing, i. e. they are necessary conditions of its kind and existence.

---

[4] Gracia, p. 17.
[5] Gracia, p. 17.

> [...] The features which a thing may or may not have, and thus are not necessary conditions for its kind or existence, are usually called "accidental".[6]

So an entity is distinguishable from other members in some respects, but in some not. Members of a group are members of a group, because they possess some similar features, but these features distinguish them also from other groups. So, it is mainly about the features a thing possess that makes it distinguishable from other things. But does this make him individual?

Indivisibility seems to be a characteristic for individuality: one entity is one thing and if you divide it, it is no more the same thing or better, you cannot divide a thing and make it two same things: "A man cannot be divided into many men and his right leg cannot be cut up into many right legs."[7] And even if you divide a certain quantity of water in some smaller quantities of water, it remains altogether the same water but none of these quantities are the same quantity of water of the original quantity of water.[8] But we could answer, that the original individual entity exists no more, but instead of that there are now some other new individual entities. Even if we cut a man into pieces, each piece is an individual entity. But altogether: the argument, that an individual has to be indivisible, does not work, because, before it is divided, the individual exists.

Gracia proposes the term 'non-instantiability' which means that an individual "cannot be instantiated as universals can".[9] There can be many men, but not many Socrates', although Socrates is a man. 'Man' is a universal, 'Socrates' is an individual. So, 'man' can divided into many men, but Socrates cannot divided into many Socrates'.

An attempt to define individuality is to equate it with 'numerical unity'. "It is called numerical because to be an individual is to be *one* thing and that involves nothing but to be a unit or [...] *a number.*[10] Opposed to this is the 'specific unity', which means all members of a species constitute an unity.

---

[6] Gracia, p. 19.
[7] Gracia, p. 23.
[8] Gracia, p. 23.
[9] Gracia, p. 24.
[10] Gracia, p. 25.

The next thing is distinction: an individual is distinct of everything else, there is nothing else, which is like itself. The question is: what draws the distinction? Especially, when two things look like the same, act same and so on, until they are equal in every single detail? What makes them different from each other? What gives them identity? So an individual is not predicable. Another thing except Socrates himself cannot be labelled as 'Socrates'. This impredicability is a further feature of an individual. Nevertheless it does not answer sufficiently the question "what makes an individual an individual".

3. Medieval Authors about the Problem of Individuation

The philosophy of individuation has its origins in the philosophy of Aristotle about the problem of universals. He tried to "define the essential nature of a thing and then to demonstrate the features the must have because of that nature."[11] Here it was not the problem of individuation but of universality, not "what distinguishes a thing from all other things?" but "what is the essence of a thing that is equal to all other things of this kind?". This universality of things of a group implies the question of the diversity of things which do not belong to the same group.

Boethius divided the universals in the two main types "genera" and "species". For Augustine and Plato, models of the single entities exist: for Plato they are the ideas in the World of Being, for Augustine they are ideas in the divine mind. But all entities are images of these abstract models, these ideas.

What is an interesting thought, and what could serve as an explanation of "what is an individual and what makes an individual an individual", is the following intuition of Augustine:

> What devout man imbued with true religion, even though he is not yet able to see these things, nevertheless is, whatever things are contained in their own genus with a certain nature of their own, so that they might exist, are begotten by God their author [...]. All things are set up by reason, and a man not by the same reason as a horse – for that is absurd to suppose. Therefore, single things are created

---

[11] McGrade, Arthur Stephen (2006): *The Cambridge Companion to Medieval Philosophy.* Cambridge: Cambridge University Press (The Cambridge Companions to Philosophy, Religion and Culture), p. 196.

with their own reasons. But where are we to think these reasons exist, if not in the mind of the creator? [...] These reasons, as was said, whether it is right to call them Ideas or forms or species or reasons, many are permitted to call [them] whatever they want, but [only] to a very few [is it permitted] to see what is true.[12]

God gave reason to every single entity, maybe this is the feature or the factor that makes an entity an individual?

Gracia answers to that:

It is argued that God, as creator of each individual substance, is related to it in a unique way and thus that owing to this relation the substance is rendered individual. The disadvantage of this theory springs from its reliance on religious authority. Its suitability depends not only on the existence of God, which is after all a topic of philosophical controversy, but on purely theological assumptions concerning creation and God's nature and will. For these reasons it cannot be, and indeed seldom has been, taken seriously as a viable philosophical alternative to the problem of individuation.[13]

Obviously Augustine's argument is not really helpful in our investigation of "what makes an individual an individual".

So let us see, what Thomas Aquinas adds to this theme. He speaks about the essence and the essence is what should denote the individuality of an individual:

A nature, however, or essence...can be considered in two ways. First, we can consider it according to its proper notion, and this is its absolute consideration; and in this way nothing is true of it except what pertains to it as such; whence if anything else is attributed to it, that will yield a false attribution...In the other way [an essence] is considered as it exists in this or that [individual]; and in this way something is predicated of it *per accidens* [nonessentially], on account of that in which it exists, as when we say that a man is white because Socrates is white, although this does not pertain to man as such.

A nature considered in this way, however, has two sorts of existence. It exists in singulars on the one hand, and in the soul on the other, and from each of these [sorts of existence] it acquires accidents. In the singulars, furthermore, the essence has several [acts of] existence according to the multiplicity of singulars. Nevertheless, if we consider the essence in the first, or absolute, sense, none of

[12] McGrade, p. 198.
[13] Gracia, p. 46.

these pertain to it. For it is false to say that the essence of man, considered absolutely, has existence in this singular, because if existence in this singular pertained to man insofar as he is man, man would never exist, except as this singular. Similarly, if it pertained to man insofar as he is man not to exist in this singular, then the essence would never exist in the singular. But it is true to say that man, but not insofar as he is man, may be in this singular or in that one, or else in the soul. Therefore, the nature of man considered absolutely abstracts from every existence, though it does not exclude any. And the nature thus considered is what is predicated of each individual.[14]

This statement is confusing. Aquinas seems to contradict himself. But he just means that the essence can be seen as a metaphysical instance which serves as a model or an idea and when this essence exists in a singular entity it "not strictly the same but recognizably the same", its content is given to this singular entity, like a copy or like the absolute essence put its mark on the singular entity. And this entity obtains some accidents which define it additionally. But my question remains: "When exactly does this entity become an individual? Already by receiving the 'stamp' of the essence or only just by receiving accidents?"

4. Conclusion

I could not answer the question of the individuality of an individual. So unproblematic it seems to be for us in our everyday life, so problematic it is to solve for the philosophy.

It will remain an issue for many generations of philosophers and it is an issue which is important for our self-conception: who are we, how are we, where do we come from. This "mystery" is an excellent example that our mind can so hard explain what our intuition knows.

---

[14] McGrade, p. 202.

5. Resources

- Drosdowski, Günther (Hg.) (1963): *Duden "Etymologie". Herkunftswörterbuch der deutschen Sprache.* Mannheim [u.a.]: Bibliogr. Inst (Der Duden in 10 Bänden, 7).
- Gracia, Jorge J. E. (1988): *Introduction to the Problem of Individuation in the early Middle Ages.* 2. Aufl. München [u.a.]: Philosophia-Verl (Analytica).
- McGrade, Arthur Stephen (2006): *The Cambridge Companion to Medieval Philosophy.* Cambridge: Cambridge University Press (The Cambridge Companions to Philosophy, Religion and Culture).